THE
BLOOD MOONS
PROPHECY,
JERUSALEM
AND
2017

BOB MITCHELL

THE
BLOOD MOONS
PROPHECY,
JERUSALEM
AND
2017

Also by Bob Mitchell

Rome, Babylon the Great and Europe

The Messiah Code

Antichrist, The Vatican and the Great Deception

The Post Tribulation Rapture of the Church

Signs of the End

All scripture quotations are from the King James Bible

Introduction

Let me begin by thanking you for purchasing this little booklet and may I state at the outset I am no prophet. Neither do I claim to know what the future holds apart from those specific events foretold in the Holy Bible: The casting out of the Jewish people from their homeland and their subsequent return in the period known as the "Last Days", events now firmly established in ancient and modern history. The coming of the Messiah before the destruction of the temple in 70AD was prophesied by Isaiah and Daniel hundreds of years before both events took place. The rise of a Revived Roman Empire is also something the ancient seers of Israel saw in visions granted them by the God of Abraham, Isaac and Jacob due to stride across the world stage in the end times followed by the rise, the rule and the eventual demise of the man known as the Antichrist at the hands of the Jewish Messiah as he returns in triumph from the heavens.

Today we live in those prophesied "Times of the End" when ancient prophecies come tumbling almost daily from the pages of our bibles onto our newspapers and TV screens.

Those who mock or ignore these times do so at their peril. The days that now lay before us will be days of unprecedented trouble and trial filled with persecution for those who love the truth and will not succumb to the ravings and lies of the Antichrist and the man who will be at his side whom the bible calls the "False Prophet".

As we enter these turbulent times the bible warns of false teachers and false prophets who will deceive many with their fake prognostications. We shall look at these failed prophecies in the pages that follow. But I wish also to place before the reader the possibility that something is indeed about to happen. If I am correct then may God prepare us for those days. If I am wrong then may God excuse me and grant us those extra days in spreading the gospel before the rise of those penultimate days before the Messiah Jesus Christ, returns in glory.

However, I feel in necessary to place before the reader some things I have discovered in my studies. Time will either prove me a fool or correct for sharing these things.

I am not saying "Thus says the Lord" or even saying in my own strength "these things will surely come to pass". I merely place what follows before the reader as a "maybe".

It is easy to say "Such and such will happen in the next year".
But many of today's so-called TV prophets flood the airwaves with predictions such as all debt being cancelled or certain members of the population being destroyed by God's fire (as has been said before) in the coming year. And when it doesn't happen they carry on as normal spewing out their false predictions and the gullible masses eat it up like babies swallowing poison. This is what the bible warned us would happen in the end times as we approach the return of the Messiah. False prophets will abound and lead many astray. But is anyone listening? Few listen but so many refuse to believe their favourite preacher would ever lie

to them. Or they use the excuse "predicting the future is like iding a bike. You fall off a few times as you learn". This is utter nonsense!

When the prophets of the bible made their predictions they had to be correct 100% of the time and no mistakes were permitted. If you were wrong you ran the distinct risk of being stoned to death for speaking lies in God's name. Not so today.

But there came a time in Israel's history when they refused to listen to God's prophets but rather enjoyed the words of the false prophets who told them of good times ahead full of blessings. The result was God's judgement upon the nation. As it was in old times when Israel went away from the Lord and listened to the lies of the false prophets so it is today. God used the prophet Jeremiah who cried out in despair:

Jer 5:31 *The prophets prophesy falsely, and the priests bear rule by their means; and my people love to have it so: and what will ye do in the end thereof?*

Today, many professing Christians who should know and understand the times through which we are passing, and should warn those around of the coming times of the Antichrist, are ignoring the warning signs and listening instead to the voices false prophets who run rampant on Christian TV. This can only mean one thing: God is about to judge not only the unbelieving world but those within the Christian Church who have blocked their ears and refused to warn of coming danger. Rather they have compromised their faith by jumping into bed with the enemies of the God of Israel. Not only do they accept false prophets and teachers, they accept as brothers and sisters those who do not believe in the bible as the word of God or in Jesus as the only way to God. There is only one word for these people: heretics. They are like the unfaithful wife who jumps into bed with anyone who passes and gives them a smile. Woe to them!

They profess a love for truth but trample it beneath their feet in their cowardly, blind rush to be all things to all men. The God of Abraham Isaac and Jacob, the God and Father of Jesus Christ sees their treachery and it will not go unchallenged in the court of heaven. The date is set, the tribunal will sit and judgement will be passed. Judgement that will be irrevocable for all eternity.

So it is with a profound sense of awe and responsibility I undertake the following. I repeat I am not a prophet. I am a student of bible prophecy and have been since my conversion to Christianity in 1962. Many of you reading this are the same as me: simple lovers of the prophetic word of God.

I dedicate the following to all those who seek truth and are not adamant in their statements but are willing to lay out their findings for their brothers and sisters in Christ to view and critique. They are willing to make mistakes and be corrected by those who are better informed as further revelation is discovered, yet pick themselves up, have the humility to apologise and with God's good grace continue to diligently study the word.

Most of all I dedicate this to my Lord, Saviour, king, and everlasting friend; the Lord Jesus Christ, Messiah of Israel, Lamb of God, the ultimate, final sacrifice for the sins of mankind, in whom alone salvation and everlasting life are found. No Angel, no Saint, no Mary, no Pope, Priest, King or any other creature in all the universe and beyond is able to rescue man from his awful sinful condition and bring him safely into the kingdom of heaven. No other name is given whereby a man may be saved...none but the name of Jesus Christ, Yeshua Ha Mashiach (Yeshua (Jesus) the Messiah).

I do hope you enjoy this little book. I haver attempted to make it as cheap to buy as possible in order that many may be able to read and even critique what is written herein. May God bless you as you serve him in these end times.

Bob Mitchell
UK 2016

CHAPTER ONE
BLOOD MOON EVIDENCE

Let's begin by asking the question "what are the blood moons"?

The blood moons in this instance are a tetrad (a series of four consecutive lunar eclipses—coinciding on Jewish holidays—with six full moons in between, and no intervening partial lunar eclipses) which began with the April 2014 lunar eclipse (Feast of Passover) and ended with the lunar eclipse on September 27-28, 2015 (Feast of Tabernacles). According to Pastors Mark Biltz and John Hagee these events signaled the onset of the end times as predicted in Acts 2:20 and Revelation 6:12.

But did they? Let's look at these predictions: Acts 2:20 says:

The sun shall be turned into darkness, and the moon into blood, before that great and notable day of the Lord come

This is a direct quote by the Apostle Peter from Joel chapter 2. Revelation 6:12 also says:

And I beheld when he had opened the sixth seal, and, lo, there was a great earthquake; and the sun became black as sackcloth of hair, and the moon became as blood.

In his book "Four Blood Moons" with the sub-heading "Something is about to change" Pastor Hagee quotes as an additional backup verse the first few words of Luke 21:25

And there shall be signs in the sun, and in the moon, and in the stars. He then misses the rest of the verse and the entire following verse: *and upon the earth distress of nations, with perplexity; the sea and the waves roaring; Luke 21:26 Men's hearts failing them for fear, and for looking after those things which are coming on the earth: for the powers of heaven shall be shaken.*

He then carries on with verses 27 and 28:

Luke 21:27-28: *And then shall they see the Son of man coming in a cloud with power and great glory. And when these things begin to come to pass, then look up, and lift up your heads; for your redemption draweth nigh.*

Perhaps pastor Hagee omitted the scriptures for brevities sake but they are important for a number of very good reasons and it does give the impression when you see the blood moon Jesus is coming soon after.

The result of the celestial signs Jesus gave will be distress of nations, men's hearts failing them because the very powers of the heavens will be affected. Did this happen during the blood moons of 2014-2015? Not at all. For the most part life on planet earth carried on as normal.

Also, we must look at just where and when Jesus spoke these words so as not to misrepresent the words of the Messiah. He said these words during what is known as the Olivet Discourse recorded also in Matthew 24 and Mark 13 and Luke 21. The place was the Mount of Olives just east of the city of Jerusalem. Jesus gave a run-down of events that would occur right up to his return in glory.
So where did Jesus place the celestial events John Hagee and others clearly suggest were the 2014-2015 tetrads of blood

moons heralding major events of the last days? Jesus the greatest prophet of all took the prophecy of Joel and the signs in the heavens and placed them nowhere other than after the Great Tribulation, the time when Antichrist will carry out his evil, demonically inspired rule.

Also, if one studies the Olivet Discourse and Revelation 6 and 7 one discovers an amazing mirror image. Remember it is the same Jesus speaking in Matthew 24 as the Jesus who opens the seals in Revelation 6 and 7.

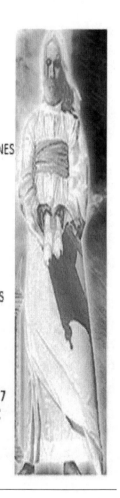

THE OLIVET DISCOURSE MATTHEW 24	THE 6 SEALS REVELATION 6
1. FALSE MESSIAHS	1. WHITE HORSE
2. WARS	2. RED HORSE: WAR
3. FAMINES	3. BLACK HORSE: FAMINES
4. DEATH	4. PALE HORSE: DEATH
5. PERSECUTION	5. MARTYRS
6. COSMIC SIGNS PEOPLE MOURN;	6. COSMIC SIGNS DAY OF HIS WRATH HAS COME;
SOUND OF A TRUMPET; CHRIST GATHERS HIS ELECT	GREAT CROWD ARRIVES IN HEAVEN OUT OF THE GREAT TRIBULATION

NEITHER IN MATTHEW 24 OR REVELATION 6/7 DO WE FIND SO MUCH AS A HINT OF COSMIC SIGNS BEFORE THE TRIBULATION. THEY TAKE PLACE AFTER THE TRIBULATION...NEVER BEFORE!

So why take a series of blood moons that take place on Jewish feast days and then take the words of Jesus himself out of context and make it seem that what you write is a fulfillment of the words of the Messiah?

When I first read of the so-called "blood moon" prophecies, like many others I was intrigued. However, my initial excitement that these celestial events may be harbingers of coming prophetic events soon vanished like early morning sea mist. I am not saying those who offered this information in books, DVDs, conference appearances and television were deliberately pulling the wool over the sheep's eyes in order to enlarge their ministries or bank accounts but they were at the very least being misled by others without testing the information for themselves.

This is very serious because while many do not have access to the internet most of us do. We certainly have access to the bible to check out the reliability of quotes given to back a preacher's words regardless of who he is. As such it is our responsibility before the Lord to "prove *all things*" 1 Thessalonians 5:21.

The Greek word translated "prove" means to test, to examine. Sadly so many of us are used to being spoon fed by the man at the front of the church that we swallow anything he or an invited speaker says or someone has said via the internet. I can remember someone arguing with me over something a while ago and their response was "Well it's on YouTube." As if YouTube is the final authority on trustworthy information. No! The Holy Bible is the final authority, not man, woman, pastor, priest or pope or even YouTube! The word of God is final. Until we get that right in our thinking we run the risk of being misled and drawn away from the truth by anyone who professes to have an inside knowledge. Always check out what you are being taught and by whom.

THE HISTORICAL "PROPHETIC" EVIDENCE FOR THE BLOOD MOONS

Is there any evidence the blood moons in the past have been portents of coming disasters or major events as Pastors Biltz and Hagee claim? Those who spin the blood moon prophecies will say yes and give a list of impressive data regarding the validity of their claims that the tetrads are indeed prophetic of some major event.

So let's check out these claims to see how they stand up to the litmus test of truth.

BLOOD MOONS 1493-1494

THE EXPULSION OF THE JEWS FROM SPAIN AND THE SAILING OF COLUMBUS

We are told by the supporters of the blood moon tetrads of 1493-1494 that they were significant due to the fact that the Jews of Spain were exiled from that country by King Ferdinand and Queen Isabella around that time.

First, let us look at a little history of the Jews in Spain. According to the leading Jewish figure of the time, Don Isaac Abrabanel, the Jews of Spain originally arrived there under the rule of a man named Pharos a Grecian, at the time of the Babylonian captivity of 597 - 538 BC. Pharos was said to have been given a kingdom in Spain. He was also said to be a friend of the king of Babylon, Nebuchadnezzar, and was given a portion of the Jewish captives which he then took to Spain by ship.

The Jewish people thrived in the land and became integrated into the culture while keeping their own ancient traditions. Later during the expulsion of the Jews by the Romans in 135 AD, many eventually arrived in Spain. Twice in Romans chapter 15 Paul mentions his plan to visit Spain. While he was the Apostle to the Gentiles it should also be remembered that almost wherever he went he made a point of entering the Synagogue of that city to speak to the Jews there. Was he desiring to speak to the Jews of Spain? We shall never know because as far as we know he never made it to Spain but was arrested and spent his last years in Rome. But it is an interesting thought, nonetheless.

The Jewish exiles in Spain who were descended by lineage from Judah, Benjamin, Shimon and Levi, according to Abrabanel, settled in two districts in southern Spain: one, Andalusia, in the city of Lucena - a city so-called by the Jewish exiles that had come there; the second, in the country around Ṭulayṭulah (Toledo). Abrabanel said that the name Ṭulayṭulah (Toledo) was given to the city by its first Jewish inhabitants, and surmised that the name may have meant טלטול (= wandering), on account of their wandering from Jerusalem. (see Wikipedia "History of the Jews in Spain")

The edict exiling all Jews from Spain.

So by the time the king and queen pronounced the decree to exile the Jewish population there must have been a very large number who were uprooted from their homes and businesses where they had lived for many years. The decree was issued on April 29, 1492, and was, in fact, the pet idea of the Catholic Inquisition under its head Father Tomas de Torquemada. All Jews were ordered to leave Spain. If they wished to convert to Roman Catholicism they were welcomed to stay. Many did convert and were later branded "Marrano" derived from an Arabic word meaning "dirty" or pig".

As we saw above, the expulsion of the Jewish people from Spain took place in 1492. So how does this tetrad of blood moons fit into pastors Hagee and Biltz's presentations?

Pastors Hagee and Biltz, as well as others, quote the edict from the king and Queen of Spain in 1492 in which all Jews were stripped of their possessions and ordered to leave Spain as being connected to the appearance of the blood moons. Some other blood mooners use the voyage of Christopher Columbus as evidence for the blood moons being in some way significant.

But hold on!!

The blood moon tetrads did not even begin to take place until a year after the edict of the King and Queen of Spain and after Columbus set sail to the Americas. So how could they be prophetic??
Prophecy means to foretell the future in this case. But unless Hagee and Biltz are prophesying in reverse this is a fogging up of the evidence. The edict against Jews as well

as the sailing of Columbus took place in 1492...the blood moons began in 1493.

So...nothing prophetic in any of the blood moons here.

I will, no doubt, make this same statement again in the future but I am bewildered as to how people who are supposed to be students of the word of God and know the prophecies in the bible can read about these moons that took place after a major Jewish event, see scriptures wrested from their context and squeezed into meaning something with which they are not meant to have any relation.

Am I missing something here?

John Hagee clearly writes on the front cover of his book "FOUR BLOOD MOONS" then in the subtext he writes "SOMETHING IS ABOUT TO CHANGE".

Pastor Hagee how can you suggest the blood moons are prophetic, because that is clearly what you are doing, when these blood moon tetrads take place AFTER the event?? That isn't prophetic, sir.

Who is being fooled here, pastor Hagee? You or your readers, congregation and listeners...or all?

BLOOD MOONS 1949- 1950
THE RE-BIRTH OF THE STATE OF ISRAEL AND THE WAR OF INDEPENDENCE

God promised the land of Israel to Abraham, Isaac, Jacob and their descendants. The land mass promised covers an area from Egypt to the Persian Gulf taking in parts of Turkey, Syria, all of Jordan, parts of Iraq and Iran and ending at the Persian Gulf. The only kingdoms ever to come close to fulfilling this promise were the kingdoms of David and Solomon.

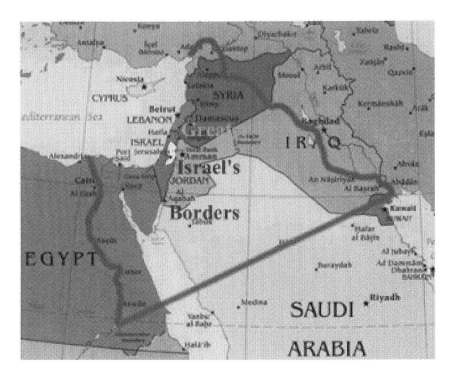

But God also warned them if they rebelled he would cast them out of the land but always with a view to bringing them back because he had promised the land to no one else but them forever.

Deut 28:63-68

63 *and it shall come to pass, that as the lord rejoiced over you to do you good, and to multiply you; so the lord will rejoice over you to destroy you, and to bring you to nought; and ye shall be plucked from off the land whither thou goest to possess it. And the lord shall scatter thee among all people, from the one end of the earth even unto the other; and there thou shalt serve other gods, which neither thou nor thy fathers have known, even wood and stone. and among these nations shalt thou find no ease, neither shall the sole of thy foot have rest: but the Lord shall give thee there a trembling heart, and failing of eyes, and sorrow of mind: and thy life shall hang in doubt before thee; and thou shalt fear day and night, and shalt have none assurance of thy life: in the morning thou shalt say, would God it were even! And at even thou shalt say, would God it were morning! For the fear of thine heart wherewith thou shalt fear, and for the sight of thine eyes which thou shalt see. And the lord shall bring thee into Egypt again with ships, by the way whereof I spake unto thee, thou shalt see it no more again: and there ye shall be sold unto your enemies for bondmen and bondwomen, and no man shall buy you.*

Moses continued with a hope of a final return to the land:

Deuteronomy 30:1-5

...and it shall come to pass, when all these things are come upon thee, the blessing and the curse, which I have set before

thee, and thou shalt call them to mind among all the nations, whither the Lord thy God hath driven thee, and shalt return unto the Lord thy God, and shalt obey his voice according to all that I command thee this day, thou and thy children, with all thine heart, and with all thy soul; that then the Lord thy God will turn thy captivity, and have compassion upon thee, and will return and gather thee from all the nations, whither the Lord thy God hath scattered thee. If any of thine be driven out unto the outmost parts of heaven, from thence will the Lord thy God gather thee, and from thence will he fetch thee: and the Lord thy God will bring thee into the land which thy fathers possessed, and thou shalt possess it; and he will do thee good, and multiply thee above thy fathers.

The Jewish people were warned by Moses that if they rebelled against the Lord he would exile them around the globe until finally he would bring them home. They did rebel and the Lord sent them to Babylon for 70 years. Then following their return they rebelled even more by finally rejecting the Messiah. Then in 70 AD the Roman Legions under Titus destroyed the Temple finally exiling the Jewish people around the world for almost 2,000 years; chased from city to city country to country resulting finally in the Holocaust of the Second World War.

When one reads many of the Psalms they can be seen to be prophetic in nature. For instance, the crucifixion of the Messiah, his being pierced and the gambling for his garments can be clearly identified in Psalm 22 when the writer states:

Psalm 22:13-18

They gaped upon me with their mouths, as a ravening and a roaring lion. I am poured out like water, and all my bones are out of joint: my heart is like wax; it is melted in the midst of my bowels. My strength is dried up like a potsherd; and my tongue cleaveth to my jaws; and thou hast brought me intothe dust of death. For dogs have compassed me: the assembly of the wicked have inclosed me: they pierced my hands and my feet. I may tell all my bones: they look and stare upon me. They part my garments among them, and cast lots upon my vesture.

Interestingly another Psalm that can be looked upon as being prophetic is Psalm 102.

As you read through this Psalm that is full of anguish and suffering, may I ask you to recall the suffering of the Jewish people through the years, especially the terrible time of the Shoah, the Holocaust.

May I draw your attention to the following verses:

Psalm 102: 13-18

Thou shalt arise, and have mercy upon Zion: for the time to favour her, yea, the set time, is come. For thy servants take pleasure in her stones, and favour the dust thereof. So the heathen shall fear the name of the LORD, and all the kings of the earth thy glory.

Now please note the last 2 verses included here:

When the LORD shall build up Zion, he shall appear in his glory. He will regard the prayer of the destitute, and not despise their prayer. This shall be written for the generation to come: and the people which shall be created shall praise the LORD.

"When the Lord shall build up Zion he shall appear in his glory" This, if prophetic, could not have been meant be linked to the return from Babylon in 538 BC for the Messiah was not to appear for more than another 500 years.

But what if we look at this as a prophecy for our day when the Jewish people finally returned home after the horrors of the Nazi Holocaust? Does it fit then?

I believe it does because verse 18 states: *This shall be written for the generation to come: and the people which shall be created shall praise the LORD.*

Incredibly, we have witnessed the return of the Jewish people to Israel after an absence of almost 2,000 years. Now following the long years of suffering, the persecutions, the pogroms, the expulsions and the Holocaust they are home again. We have witnessed a miracle almost equal to the parting of the Red Sea. A people divorced from their land for almost 2 millennia have against all odds returned and thrived even though surrounded by their enemies and having been forced to defend themselves several times against overwhelming forces. They could so easily have been driven into the sea but for the hand of God in the world's affairs.

Now, the phrase "This shall be written for the generation to come..." is extremely interesting. The words translated here as "the generation to come" is not what the Hebrew actually says. The Hebrew says "dor acharon". These words should send a shiver of excitement down every believer's spine and a glow of hope in their heart because they really mean "This is written for *the last generation*."

We have here, a Psalm that relates not only to the Holocaust of World War Two but to the return of the Jewish people to their homeland. But more than this, the Hebrew then tells us plainly "When the Lord shall build up Zion (Israel) he shall appear in his glory...this is written for the last generation!"

Have the Jewish people returned to their homeland? Absolutely. This must mean those who saw the re-birth of the State of Israel will see the Lord appear in glory because it goes on to tell us "this is written for the last generation." The words could not be clearer. Now that is the bible, the plain, prophetic word of God clearly shown. But what do our friends who promote the blood moons tell us?

On May 14, 1948, Israel became a nation once again after vanishing for almost 2,000 years from every map in the world. Our blood moon proponents tell us the blood moons began on Passover 1949.

In order to salvage some respectability for their case they tell us it was during this time of the blood moons Israel was fighting for her existence. Unfortunately, for them, the first blood moon of the tetrad began one month after the armistice was signed between Israel and her Arab neighbours in March, 1949. The tetrad began on April 13th (Passover). Did you get that? Israel and the Arabs ended hostilities one month before the first blood moon of the tetrad. How can that be significant? What does that predict? The war had been over for a month before the moon even showed signs of turning blood red!!

Do you see how easily Christians swallow this without even checking it out? Is God pleased with our laziness, our lack of discernment? It must crush our father's heart to see his children open their hearts and minds to things so easily proven to be of no value.

Not only are they of no scriptural significance, but Jesus, himself never even mentioned them. The only time he mentioned a blood moon, that we should take note of, is not due to appear until AFTER the Tribulation. Yet we swallow and praise the words of those who rip the scriptures out of context to prove their claims.

We should be rightly dividing the word of God in these days. May God wake us up in these end times to truly study his word and test every spirit.

BLOOD MOONS 1967-1968
THE 6 DAY WAR

It was the morning of June 5, 1967. For months, Egyptian President Gamal Abdul Nasser had been boasting and threatening the annihilation of the State of Israel. Lebanese newspapers ran a cartoon showing Nasser kicking the Israelis into the Mediterranean Sea. Syria and Iraq also had been sabre rattling and preparing their troops for the coming conflict.

Lebanese Newspaper Al-Farida, showing Nasser kicking the "Jew," Israel, into the sea, with the armies of Lebanon, Syria and Iraq supporting him.

Israel wasted no time as the threat reached its peak on June 4th. Egypt had 343 aircraft ready to attack the little Jewish State. At 07:45 a.m. on the morning of June 5th Israel launched a pre-emptive strike against Egypt. By late morning, Egypt had been left with just 35 operational aircraft. And by noon the combined air forces of Jordan and Syria had also been all but wiped out.

Just 6 days later on June 10th, the fighting was over. Israel had not only extended her territory in the north and east but for the first time since the rule of the Roman legions, she was in sole possession of her ancient capital, Jerusalem.

Surely if there was anything worthy of being called prophetically significant, the recapture of Jerusalem was it.

And guess what? The first blood moon of the tetrad appeared on Passover, April 24, 1967. Almost 2 months before the war began.

At last, we have a winner!

So does that mean the blood moons are indeed prophetic? Not at all.

We have looked, so far, at 3 sets of blood moon tetrads.
That is 12 blood moons, 3 sets of 4.

How many of these blood moons appeared before a major Jewish event?

Just 1!!

This means 11 blood moons out of 12 had no prophetic significance whatsoever. They all appeared at least a year after the event. It stuns me when I see how many websites, books, DVDs, YouTube videos, conferences and TV interviews have been based on the blood moons when out of 12 moons the "prophecy experts" claim are portents only 1 actually appeared before a major historic event!

But what about the much-heralded blood moon tetrads of 2014-2015? Were they prophetic in any way?

As of the time of writing, March 2016, we have seen no significant event to do with Israel in any way. We must remember according to the promoters of the blood moons, the tetrads are linked to the nation of Israel and the Jewish people.

The last of the recent blood moon tetrads took place on the feast of Tabernacles, September 28, 2015. It has now been several months and so far...nothing! Will we receive an apology from the experts?

You may think I am being unkind to write in this way but I am so concerned about my brothers and sisters in Christ being deceived in these times. Even by well-meaning preachers / teachers. And it concerns me greatly to wonder, if people can be so undiscerning they give their God-given cash and time to statements that can be proven to have no scriptural basis, what will people do when the great deceiver, Antichrist appears?

So do we trust the word of God when it says the blood moon (not moons) will appear after the tribulation, and surrounded by accompanying cosmic and earthly signs?

Or do we believe the "teachers" who point to 4 sets of 4 blood moons from the years 1493-1494; 1949-1950; 1967-1968; 2014-2015 and out of the entire run of 16 blood moons only 1 occurred before a major event in Jewish history?

Now, you may shoot me down in flames in the coming days

but I now wish to present to you certain patterns in recent Jewish and Gentile history that may (please note I wrote "may") have significance for the world and especially the Jewish and Arabic peoples in the years ahead.

CHAPTER TWO

JUBILEE YEARS AND 2017

I write the following with an air of trepidation. If I am wrong in what I write I promise to appear on my YouTube channel (shofar ministries) and make a public apology. I will also place the apology on Facebook and on my blog (http://www.shofar-ministries.blogspot.co.uk/) and in my church.

JUBILEE YEARS AND THE YEAR 2017

What I am about to share with you I share as an aid to study. It is not a prophecy. It is something to consider and watch just what, if anything, takes place in the coming days.

Many people come on the scene today and claim to be a prophet or seer, one who can tell what is going to happen. More often than not their predictions fall flat.

So what I offer is NOT a prediction as such. It is an anomaly that I find very interesting. At the moment, that is all it is very interesting The coming days and years will prove whether what I offer here has any validity at all.

As many will know numbers are very important to biblical scholars and to the ancient writers of the Bible.
One such number is 50.

After 49 years were completed and Israel entered the 50th year certain things were due to occur such as the releasing of debts and so on.

Notice: it is after the 49th year, during the 50th year, not after 50 years these and other things were to take place. So certain events were to take place during the 50th year.

I found it fascinating, to say the least when I began to study this in light of us now living in what many believe to be the last days prior to the physical return to earth of Jesus Christ. The Bible predicts in several places the Jewish people would return to their ancient homeland in "the last days" or "end of days".

So let's spend a few minutes looking at the 50 year cycle in light of Israel and the Jews return.........

The first date we shall look at is 1897. In 1897, the very first Zionist Conference was held in Basle Switzerland with a view to finding a homeland for the scattered Jewish people who had been spread around the world since their expulsion from the land of Israel by the Roman armies in 135 A.D.
It was only after this expulsion the Romans renamed the land Syria Palestina (Palestine).

So we take 1897 as our start date.........

1897 THE VERY FIRST ZIONIST CONFERENCE SEEKING A HOMELAND FOR THE JEWISH PEOPLE

First Zionist Conference 1897

Interestingly Theodore Herzl who led the movement stated he may not live to see the Jewish state but within 50 years it would be a reality. How close he was!

We then add 49 years to 1897 and the 50th year is 1947.

1947 THE UN VOTES IN FAVOUR OF THE CREATION OF THE STATE OF ISRAEL

1897 + 50= 1947, The newly formed UN votes in favour of a homeland for the Jews in Palestine.

RESOLUTION 181

The partition plan was approved by 33 to 13, with 10 abstentions.

The 33 countries that cast the "Yes" vote were: Australia, Belgium, Bolivia, Brazil, Byelorussia, Canada, Costa Rica, Czechoslovakia, Denmark, Dominican Republic, Ecuador, France, Guatemala, Haiti, Iceland, Liberia, Luxembourg, Netherlands, New Zealand, Nicaragua, Norway, Panama, Paraguay, Peru, Philippines, Poland, Sweden, Ukraine, Union of South Africa, USSR, USA, Uruguay, Venezuela. (Among other countries, the list includes the US, the three British Dominions, all the European countries except for Greece and the UK, but including all the Soviet-block countries.)

The 13 countries that chose the Hall of Shame and voted "No" were: Afghanistan, Cuba, Egypt, Greece, India, Iran, Iraq, Lebanon, Pakistan, Saudi Arabia, Syria, Turkey, Yemen. (Ten of these are Moslem countries; Greece has the special distinction of being the only European country to have joined the Hall of Shame.)

The ten countries that abstained are: Argentina, Chile, China, Colombia, El Salvador, Ethiopia, Honduras, Mexico, United Kingdom, Yugoslavia.

United Nations

We then carry on and add 49 years to 1947 and the 50th year is 1997.

 1947+50= 1997.

1997 THE FIRST EVER PAN ARABIC CONFERENCE WITH A VIEW TO RECAPTURING JERUSALEM

In this 50th year the very first ever pan-Arabic Conference was held with a view to recapturing the land of Israel and especially the city of Jerusalem.

That is interesting: every 50 years a major conference regarding the Jewish people and their homeland.

But did you notice:
1st Conference: held by Jews.
2nd Conference: held by the Gentile nations
3rd Conference: held by the Arab nations

Three major conferences held by three distinct groups, Jews, Gentiles and Arabs. Each one taking place 50 years apart.

1897+50= 1947+50= 1997
<u>JERUSALEM MYSTERY</u>

But there is something very similar regarding the city of Jerusalem. Our start date here is 1917 when after 500 years of Turkish rule Palestine was captured by the British toward the end of the First World War.

<u>1917 THE BRITISH EMPIRE ENDS THE 500 YEAR RULE OF THE OTTOMANS AND LIBERATES JERUSALEM FROM TURKISH RULE</u>

1917 the Ottoman Empire falls and Great Britain takes control of Palestine. General Allenby (a Christian) walks into the city rather than on horseback.

General Allenby entering the Jaffa Gate, Jerusalem, 1917

1917+50= 1967.

THE 6 DAY WAR AND THE RECAPTURE OF JERUSALEM

We now add 49 years to 1917 and during the 50th year of 1967, during the June Six Day War, Israel captured the Old City of Jerusalem for the first time in over 2,000 years.

Israeli troops preparing to enter Jerusalem June 1967

There is a sequence here:
1st war: Gentiles capture Jerusalem
2nd war: Jews capture Jerusalem

Two major wars in which the centre prize is Jerusalem. Each war 50 years apart.

First, the Gentiles capture Jerusalem.
Second, the Jews capture Jerusalem.

But there is now another anomaly.....
All these events run in a 20 and 30 year cycle:
1897+20=1917+30=1947+20=1967+30=1997

If the pattern holds true the next date is 2017.

Which is 20 years from 1997 but strangely enough is
50 years from the Six Day War of 1967.

It is also 120 years from the first ever Zionist conference.

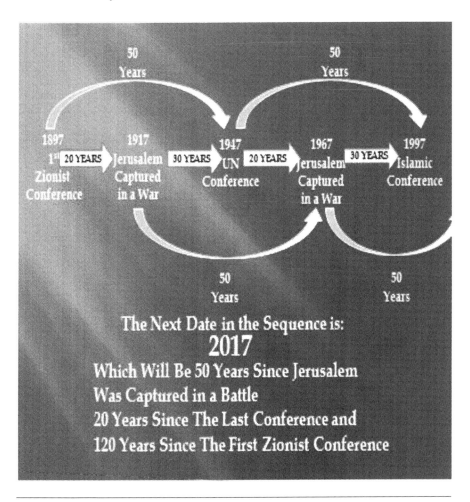

God said in Genesis_6:3 *And the LORD said, My spirit shall not always strive with man, for that he also is flesh: yet his days shall be an hundred and twenty years.*
One wonders since the Jewish people actively began to seek a way to return to their homeland has Israel's God been striving, calling men to repentance for a final 120 years or so?

We have seen 3 major conferences but only 2 major wars in the sequence.

In the first two wars, the ancient city of Jerusalem was captured first by the Gentile nations led by the British.
Then, secondly by the Jews.

Will the next war, if there is one in 2017, be one championed by the Arabs and be centered around Jerusalem in the 50th year after the 6 Day War?

Time alone will tell. We wait and watch………

ANOTHER 2017 ANOMALY

THE WOMAN OF REVELATION 12 WILL APPEAR OVER JERUSALEM IN 2017.

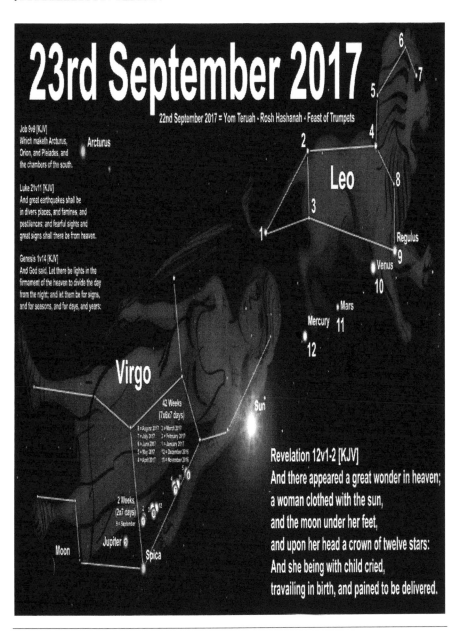

On September 23rd, 2017 a sign will appear over Jerusalem....a cosmic sign... an astrological sign according to the ancient way of observing the heavenly constellations. The sign of the virgin "betulah" in Hebrew, "Virgo" in modern language, with the sun at the centre, the moon at her feet and a crown of 12 stars above her head. At the same time, the serpent constellation will be at her feet as if ready to attack the king star Jupiter as it exits the "womb" of betulah. This is an extremely rare event; the last occurrence was 7,000 years ago. I wondered just what it signifies as it is a direct depiction of the heavenly sign predicted in the book of Revelation chapter 12 just as the tribulation and the reign of Antichrist begin on earth. The date September 23rd is the beginning of the Jewish New Year, Rosh Hashanah or the Feast of Trumpets.

Also, I went to a site that calculates the distance between dates. I discovered that 1260 days before September 23rd, 2017 there was a great Sabbath before the Passover of 2014 when the book of the prophet Malachi was read from verse 4 to 24. However in our English Bibles, we have only 18 verses of Malachi chapter 3. We then go into chapter 4. The Hebrew Bible has no chapter 4. The 6 verses of chapter 4 are verses 19 to 24 of the Hebrew book of Malachi, chapter 3. They speak of the coming day of the Lord's judgment and the arrival of Elijah the prophet before the Day of the Lord begins.

Malachi 4:5: *Behold, I will send you Elijah the prophet before the coming of the great and dreadful day of the LORD:*

Does this mean Antichrist will also appear? Could it mean that 2017 will herald the oncoming final years of Daniel's 70th week as God makes one last call to men to repent?

I have no idea. What I have shared here could be a simple anomaly. But I do believe we are most definitely in the end of days before the coming of the Lord Jesus to rule and reign. I have no idea if what I have presented will result in being any or no better than the prognostications of the blood moon purveyors.

I do feel it is correct before the Lord to at least present this to you for your own study with much prayer. At the very least I hope this stimulates you to be watchful and discerning in all your dealings with the word of God.

Jesus Christ really did come to earth and die and rise from the dead. He did this because all humanity stands guilty of cosmic treason before God.

God who is holy cannot stand sin in his glorious presence. We live with sin / cosmic treason every day. We see it on our TV screens, in our cinemas, newspapers, books and in our everyday living and moving among people who just like us flout God's eternal laws. Man thinks nothing of it because this rebellion is ingrained within him. So we all stand condemned. The sentence is eternal separation from all that is good in God's coming kingdom. That separation will be eternal and full of regret. Believe me, those who tell you they want to go to hell and party are fools, blind fools. The coming judgment will be anything but a party. It will be beyond your worst nightmare.

Why?

Because Jesus came, and when he died on the cross and rose again from the dead he did it for you. To pay for your rebellion and mine someone had to take the wrap in our place. God loves you so much and Jesus loves you so much he came and lived a pure sinless life and then went to the cross in your place and said "Father, on this cross I take the punishment that should be Joe's and Jean's and Harry's and Lucy's and everyone who ever and will ever live. I stand in their place." Yes, Jesus hung on the cross taking the full force of the punishment you and I deserve.

If you get nothing else from this booklet please leave with this: on the cross, God treated Jesus as if he were you, vile dirty rebellious and deserving of nothing but the wrath and judgment of a holy God. He did this so if you repent and follow him he could treat you as if you were Jesus, pure holy and completely sinless because Christ on the cross became your substitute..

I pray that you will turn your life over to Jesus Christ now without delay. Ask him to forgive your sins, agree with him that you are lost without his sacrifice on the cross for you. You can't do so many good deeds that they will outweigh the bad. It doesn't work like that.

That would be like the kid who jumped into mud puddles on the way home from school but still thought he could be okay when his father saw him because only his shoes and socks were dirty. God allows no sin into heaven. Only the death and the blood of Jesus Christ can clean you from your sin and guilt. Please consider these things. Time is surely running out and life is not forever. No-one leaves the planet alive only those believers who are still alive when Jesus returns to gather his own at the end. You can have the assurance of sins forgiven and a life to come with Christ in glory. What craziness it would be to say no to Christ and face an eternity of painful everlasting regret instead of joy, peace and happiness forever.

You can be made new today.

2 Corinthians 5:17 says: *Therefore if any man be in Christ, he is a new creature: old things are passed away; behold, all things are become new.*

May God guide and keep you as we await the return of our dear Lord Jesus Christ.

Contact Bob Mitchell:

bobmitchell777@yahoo.com

Blog; http://www.shofar-ministries.blogspot.co.uk

YouTube: Shofar Ministries

Printed in Great Britain
by Amazon